NEVERLASTING

Collected by Nina Loard

Published by Fiery Verse, LLC

ISBN: 978-0-9864270-1-5

Cover Art by Indie Designz

FOREWORD

Who among us hasn't loved and lived through the consequences?
Who hasn't wanted someone they can't have? Who hasn't lost someone?

There is much written about everlasting love. Odes, centuries old, celebrating two perfectly matched souls. Countless romance novels, all ending in wedding bells, the happily-ever-afters of our beloved faerie tales. But what of imperfect love?

The first flicker of lust. That final kiss. The meandering path between our beginnings and ends. In some ways, unfulfilled love may run deeper than any other kind. We carry it with us, even in the best of times. It makes us vulnerable. It makes us human. And, in some divine irony, experiencing it once, however fleeting and painful, is what compels us to try again and again.

The writers featured in this contemporary collection have captured the essence of love, loss and want in few words through dazzling displays of heart. They come from various backgrounds and countries, but all speak the same language with regards to passionate poetry. It's an honor to share them here.

In addition, several of the poets regularly take to the stage as performance artists and speak their words, bringing poetry to life in ways typeface cannot. To read a poem and experience it on a personal level is what hooks us all. To have poetry read to us as the author hears it, adds a new layer of meaning and connection. I am pleased to offer both experiences for many of the featured poems in the enhanced e-book version of this collection.

Some of the writers featured here post their creations daily and often create poetry through word-prompt challenges to keep their quills sharp. See the 'The Writers' section on how to connect with them or how to become more involved with writing poetry through social media. The following poem was one of many created from the title of this collection for #FieryVerse and chosen for feature here.
A perfectly imperfect way to begin...

Neverlasting

Had not the ink dried

on our Ever After?

Were not the pages, carefully bound,

set and sealed within our Tale?

I fear the sentiments

have run,

Once Upon the next,

to end, smudged,

Neverlasting

Todd Rokholm

TABLE OF CONTENTS

DEDICATION

For the poets

I have come to know

Come to love

And for any heart

That ever

Broke

Nina Loard

Never Meet

The most beautiful hearts

I'll never meet

Beat

Here

SubtleHoney

NEVERLASTING

Technicolor

I used to dream it was over

It was always the same

The way the color drained from the sky

How sound slowed and dulled

And the world was mute and muted

As my mouth couldn't quite form your name

Shocking how different the reality

The way everything continues in Technicolor

Surround sound without recognition

A denial that you are gone

And a strange expectation

That I will just go on

Louise Arrowsmith

Petal

Scattered

On the wind

Like seeds and spores

My love can never be

Completely yours

It snags in certain places

And disparately

Blooms

Roger Litherland

Colors of Fire

I slide my way up your thigh
as I glisten in this new heat

my skin lay crumpled at your feet
scarred and torn
a shadow of old loves

slithering over moans
and growing desire
I find your mouth ready for my sinking teeth
and fiery tongue

we writhe together
locked in a kiss
tightening our grips
sharing one breath

I am born here as are you

your pulse becomes mine
entwined as our hands paint each other
in colors of fire

Susan Purr

Mangled Stars

In the candid light of abandoned love, a soul afire

Through the mirror flaked, seeps crackled desire

Hearts beating, echoing about the room

Naked passions exposed, in a heavy burden

Our frailties weeping under the moon

If only I had paused among the shadows

Each glimmer of light on your curves, the blows

To my conscience, the now crumbling rock

Torn apart, my essence exposed in ragged clothes

Pummeled again by your indifference, there's the knock

What have I gained in this tragic bind?

The mangle of stars, cluttering my mind

That love we had cupped in a tender embrace

Now withering, its remnants lost in winter's snows

Where I will lie

To let the blizzard bury my frozen grace

Jim C. Mackintosh

Apart

Lying here

And my words

Upon the ceiling

I write

Tracing the letters

In the air above me

Do you lie there

Reading the rain as it falls?

Todd Rokholm

Dream

Your kiss tastes like deceit

Your touch seems a lie

I roll away from you in bed at night

So I cannot hear you whisper sweet untruths

Or see your face light up

As she enters your

Dream

Elsie Rose

Silhouette

I watched her silhouette

In the green glow of evening light

Imagined the lace of freckles

Draped across her back

Inhaled the tumble of blue hair

Spilled over her shoulders

I reached around

Felt her fullness

She molded to me gentler than any cloud

Has ever drifted across a sea-night sky

I was a whisper

A ghost, a vapor

Nebulous as the night

Morning came and so the solemn cold

I touched the grey stone

Her Celtic cross

Split light

John Feaster

Oak & Fire

I am an oak rooted in dry pasture

And you, a glowing ember

Free upon the wind

I love you

And you destroy me

Kevin Hulit

Embers

She refused to believe

a poem could ever be written

about her

until she danced

among violet embers

of his love

her soul afire

George Mat

Clock Strikes

Could there be a greater hole
Than that of the human soul?
When they reach right in with their hands
And pull out whatever they can
Grabbing, just grabbing
It's a bloody, sullied cleansing
Only lovers have
Hardened by each twist and turn
Why do we keep going?
Doing it again and again
Perhaps we chase that part of ourselves
For which there is no redemption
No healing, despite good intention
I do not consider myself an angry soul
But a realistic one
I know that love is just another
Of life's poisons
Sometimes quick with mercy
And at times slow, enjoying the kill
And even I, yes, I know I will love, I will

One day I will have nothing left of me

To give to him or me

So I'll climb that tower

See the magnificent hands

Of our beloved clock

And lose myself

Somewhere between 12 and 2 o'clock

No one will mourn for me

No lovers will remember my passion

No friends will be moved by my words

Only the eerie silence

A clock strikes

One less broken soul

In the world

Bambie Wodkins

With You

I won't ever see your face

Watch light dance in your eyes

Hear your laughter

Or your voice say my name

I won't ever bask in your radiant smile

Or feel your lips against mine

I won't ever hold your hand

Or feel your fingers skate circles across my skin

I won't ever hear your whispers

Or have you pull me close

Or feel you curl your body around mine

So I give the only gift I have

My heart, my soul

Breathing life into ink spilled words

So if only for a moment

I am with you

M. B. Stephens

My Conviction

Every conviction

of why I am here,

is steadily eclipsed

by your gaze.

Now I stand,

truly convicted,

sealed with the grip

of Aphrodite's ways

My sentence cast down,

the only fair penance...

To swim in your eyes,

search for your shores and

finally drown in your waves.

I suddenly gasp, as the light shines through!

My moment of ending,

is my beginning with you.

Ben Foxx

Grace

Effortless grace in her movements

Contentment beams from gentle smiles

Hypnotized for awhile

I snap out of the trance

Bustling sound fades back in

Roger Litherland

Tears

Grasped by Death's too-eager claws

From my outstretched arms

Callous fate ripped us apart

With nary a backward glance

Leaving me naught

But the sting

Of tears

Carol Drummond

Soft Torment

Torment me. Surrendered, yet resisting
With your porcelain curves and fragrant heaves
Nuzzled in the layers of where budding jewels
Treasures swelling the hug of your solitude
As if nothing has existed before or beyond
The pass of hours of sullen beauty, unforgiving
Amid the frosted firmament of season lost
This soft torment that we bargained, sealed
With a lover's kiss beneath the dancing limes
Before the treadmill of winter's ambitions turned
To nudge the shoulders of amber days against
The drift of snow whispering about your curves
I have hunkered down by the murmured blaze
To weave the fabric of dreams for tomorrow

Jim C. Mackintosh

Trouble

Seeking trouble in the form of lust

Looking for a woman or man

With a little fire in their stride

Searching for hips that don't shake

But sway with intent

For eyes that look into my darkness

And widen with excitement

Ashley Marie Egan

You

You taught me how to love

About hope in silent nights of longing

When I am feeling blue

It is this you

I remember

Jeffrey M. Kirn

Peace

My heart chases your joy

My hands long to trace and mimic your hope

My soul longs to know the freedom that you live

Even within the constraints of this world

I see you contemplate with wonder

Absorb air like it was more than oxygen

But rather a potent drug that propels growth

Catalyzes the mind and yet calms the soul

For in truth, I should not long for your peace

I yearn for my own

But I cannot help but see yours

And want it too

So I will search and fight, just like you

For more

Jacquie Roberts

Hands Clasped

Winter's breath

Through my glacial mood

Catches me

Frozen

Between bound and boundless

Hands with worlds

Clasped

Between them

Jonathan Yungkans

Midnight

It was a rendezvous

Inside a lovers' tryst

where the melody of our hearts

sings in tune

to the cry of nightingales

a place where love reaches slowly

like the succulent grape vine

under a Mediterranean

summer blue

where we stay entwined

inside the grasp of our hands

when we make love

to the rolling waves of midnight

a rendezvous

in dream

George Mat

Leviathan and the Tempest

You come at me violently, like gale to mast

The winds of this cold front I've weathered before

I fight the nature of your approach

I war with your natural force

Whether or not I can steer into your power

I fight to win, and to an end

When we drift away in the peace

From our equal obliteration

Kevin Hulit

Jester

Your eyes told me everything

Full of lies and misconception

Saying I love you

A million times

A condescending untruth

A fool you made of me

And in the end

This jester turns in her hat of colors

Wearing instead a cloak of black

In mourning for

My broken heart

Suzanne Caldwell

Coffee

I skip breakfast

And go straight

For the flesh

Probably

It's in

The way you

Take your coffee

Jeffrey M. Kirn

Real

The blush on her cheek

When he caught her

Adoring him

The glint in his eye

When they kissed

How she wished

It had all been real

Cate Derham

This Word

I neither pardon you

Nor this simple sound

When you whisper it

When anyone whispers it

I am convicted, imprisoned

Accursed by it

I need more than it

More than this word

I need cause to bestow this neck to its noose

Reason to dance naked through a baying crowd

As tepid persecutors tell of a bitter man

Walking to the gallows

Love? Scream it

Now you recognize me

Judge and Jury

Kenneth Jordan

Warm Rain

Almost wanting to pull away

But pleasure flouted pain

Insatiable

Ravenous

Bucking and heaving

She came

Like a wave

Of warm rain

Roger Litherland

Waiting

Behind cafe windows opaque with steam

She sits alone adrift in a sea of connection

Laughing voices rise above the grinding of coffee beans

Staring at the door

Heart raw with longing

The bitter taste of stolen moments

The desperate need for more

Karen Ohren

Frost

A love once strong

Now cold and broken

My sorrowed shame

This deep-set frost can't thaw

Despite the stoking

Of a desperate flame

Anne Hayward

No Words

I stop my pen

Muddled in an 'I Miss You' poem

I question this futility

For what words

Could ever bring you

Back to me?

Tara Fleur

Beloved

Night sky conceals heart and soul

as stars spark in celebration

of inflaming touches offered freely.

We have explored every dark, twisted trail

with trust and enthusiasm.

Ours has been a midnight addiction

as we have taken one another by force.

There is great love in us

but partner though you are

and forever friend

I long for a heart magic

that will begin us again.

A dream-making of completeness

a passion more of our true selves than our bodies.

Perhaps then eternity would smile kindly

and I would be your beloved.

Laura Lee Sweet

Habit

How did you survive?

I didn't.

Each moment was death

And an awakening onto death

And I stood before you as bones

Lost in the habit of walking

Todd Rokholm

Stillness of Snow

You are my nourishment

A day without you is a day I starve

A glimpse feeds me

My eyes

Devouring your rugged lines

Of endless beauty

You bring breath to my blood

Make the air lighter

So know, if you stay away too long

I will fade like fallen leaves

Waiting to be covered with

The stillness

Of snow

Catherine LoFrumento

Knife

Who holds the light,

to cut through

your choking, heart's vessels?

These soft nights,

when all one can do,

is stare out the window

waiting.

Ben Foxx

Blind

The fires of Hell eternal

Knives of pain and agony

The validation

Of a solitary tear

Blind love

I fell for

You

A. M.

Staccato

Rose crush smudge

On your collar

Faint notes of her

At the base of your throat

Staccato sound

Of my heart's

Crack

Elsie Rose

Remnants

This dark lonely night

Filled with searing tendrils of heartache

Burn my eyes with glassy memories of love that once was

And I shiver in my nightgown of lace and rejection

Sleep eluding me as the ashen moon chases the unforgiving dawn

A dawn that I wish would never come

For the glare of sunlight incinerates

The shattered remnants

Of my heart

Julie Matondi Doucet

Broken

How far can a man bend before he breaks?

When his hard exterior is explored

By a skilled surveyor

By a fatalistic player

Whose game is to chart the male terrain

Marking points of weakness

Learning portals of access

Targeting tender ground

Only a discriminating eye

Could ever see

She is predator

She is hungry

And she has found me

I, who was impenetrable,

Succumbed to the subtle venom

Injected by her touch

By each "I love you so much"

I have been conquered

By cunning in each word

She's ever spoken

I have been

Broken

Okiethyme

The Tale of the Heartbeat in the Rain

The Rain will not allow me to sleep...

nor do I want it to.

I listen to every single beat of the eternal drum...

The codes, hidden swirls.

I think of the dancer,

swaying through sheets of

blanketed tears from above.

I see her there,

shining moonlight,

glistening off every drop.

I run,

to see if I can catch

a glimpse of her,

knowing full well

she is already gone,

into the permanent corridors

of my steel-door mind.

Ben Foxx

Eating a Bleeding Sun

The Queen of Sorrow borrows light from any sun that bleeds;
It sputters and shudders and leaks in the gutters,
all while she slowly feeds.
A table of cards with hands dealt and knees knelt at her altar.
I'm praying for a royal flush, a rush, a dream;
Just one more night with the Queen.
So, drain the bright blood from my shining sphere,
watch the ichor flow like sick sanguine honey.
Drink up, Love, for the death of a star
is simply a new beginning.

Zak Cowell

Crimson

Do not speak of me and love

When all you do is wear the blood

Squeezed by your hand

From my heart

The crimson drops

Dried on the

Wound

Kevin Hulit

Aroused

There are so many things that arouse my senses

As a woman, composer, poetess

The way the gentle breeze is dancing with my curls

When the sun kisses the ocean at the horizon

Words left in the universe for me to find them

His voice rolling my name between the tongue and lips

The way I spread my arms feeling the tingle in my fingers

The passion in me that never lets me stand still

And the need to love, to please, to make possible my dreams

I wake up every morning

And go to sleep every night

Aroused by life

Vlada Mars

Unknown Faces

She tried to hide

Her fears and doubts

Among the unknown faces

In the crowd

She walked the empty streets

And lit a candle

Against the

Dark

Cate Derham

Two Hands

My left hand along the curve of your hip

My right reaching from beneath you

To cradle your chin

Arching you to catch my breaths

Upon the bare nape of your neck

The taste of your skin

Fragrance of flesh

Salty, honeyed nectar

Dizzying my head

The yearning to be deeper inside of you

In every way

Farther than anyone has ever been

That is the closest I will ever come

To feeling immortal

And holding divinity

In my two hands

Biff Rushton

Disappear

Will you disappear with me

inside the melody

of a lonely snowflake

while we sit

beneath our pine tree

and watch

this rhapsody

fall?

George Mat

Color Me Deadly

Give me a break

For pity's sake

A rest from all your devilry

You raise soot-colored rainbows

Across my blue skies

Freeze over my lakes of reserve

You're like a sore tooth

I can't stop touching

I'm addicted to your machinations

Color me deadly with blinding shards

Your spells

Your deviations

Roger Litherland

The One

From a distance

High above and far below

You've always been The One

Countless tears these eyes have seen

On silent nights

As fallen stars, restless leaves

Beneath my feet

The rise and fall of Love unknown

You'll never know the taste of me

Or the sin we would create

To speculate what could have been

A chance I'll never take

I walk away

From one true love

The one that never was

No matter how waves pass on distant shores

My heart beats painfully forevermore

And you'll always be the one

A. M.

Pearls

You took my heart

Out into deep water.

On a whim

You dropped it in

To see if it would swim,

Watched it sink

Into the dark,

While I waved my arms and sobbed,

Watched its brightness dim

Beyond the reach of the sun,

Its blues and fiery reds

Extinguished,

Down in the colorless land,

Where shadows fall and never rise,

And where even the pearls

Are black.

Jane Dougherty

Reckoning

What mark

of a Man,

of a Woman,

will be beholden,

to the one

who weeps

for them?

Ben Foxx

Luscious

A pause so luscious

I bit the words gently from his lips

to savor the sweetness

of unspoken love

A sin to be

Repeated

Susan Purr

Token

This man, once entire,

With aspirations for you

Is left broken

As your cold token of betrayal fell

Into his wishing-well

Okiethyme

Mute

On the day that I run out of words
Know that Death has made a mute of me
But that I raised Hell and waged a war
To speak one more, "I love you."

Kevin Hulit

Three Words

I love you

Three words said too often

Easily spoken, easily taken away

Meaning becomes blurred

Hearts shatter with pain

Unknowing cause

Deadening effect

We become encased

In a cast-iron cocoon

Protecting the fragility

Of a mending heart

Comfort found

In the searching of the self

Realizing worth

Knowing true value

Whole now, complete

Living, ready for love

Ready to embrace

Standing strong, empowered

Vowing never again

Surrendering to words spoken

Promises made, promises broken

Until once again ... I love you

Three words said too often

Camille Wylde

War

Every surge of lust was met by its equal

Clawed fingers were prisoned in strong hands

Writhing bodies grappling

There was nothing of love in our coupling

It was an all-out battle for control

That neither of us wanted to win, but couldn't surrender to

So we made war, not love

Until we couldn't fight anymore

Bloody, bruised

Both triumphant

L. Ruben Willis

Heart Rain

Steady rain on a heart

Soft torment

Returns

Each time I begin to forget

You

Drum

Louder

SubtleHoney

Ripples

I walk alone to the lake

and in the glass-like calm

your reflection still appears

as clear as the desert oasis

from where you stole my soul

and when the wind blows ripples

through the calm waters

I remember the time

you held my hand

and wished for your smile

to find me well

I remember often

George Mat

Trapped

He wrote of sorrow

And she drank his tears

Each word shone with such veracity

How cruel a world

To taste the lips of heaven

But to leave you to hunger

For a destiny never to be

Space and time irrelevant

To the prevalence of love

She caressed those pages

To feel the breath of his soul

In every grain of parchment

Exposed and alone she lay

Cradled in the promise of a blue moon

Trapped in shadowed illusions

Trapped in the pages

Of his heart

Amarie Molina

She Wishes to Forget

To slip away into the gentle night,
Beyond the jagged edges of the day,
Where shadows drift deep and soft beneath a starry sky
And sleep the sleep that soothes all pain away,
To sleep and hope that there will be no dreams
Of all the sweetness once we had and lost,
To sink into the dark and leave behind
The howling memories, bleak as winter frost.
For later, when the shadows fade away,
And the watchful stars sink with the setting moon,
Among the golden clouds that hide the breaking day,
Wait tomorrow's lean and hungry wolves.

Jane Dougherty

Caged

You steal the air from burning lungs

Breathless

As your eyes devour

The essence

Of this fluttering soul

Caged by your desire

Karen Ohren

The Notes in the Tides

There you were...so many years,

our beginnings, reborn crystal.

You saw me, corner of your eye.

The tides, how they would pull.

Things evolve, people change, that look, never tame.

Hidden streams, moonlit nights, fireflies our witness.

The movements, craving silhouettes...

uncaged beasts, clawing at time, a fast illusion,

motion of emotions, trembling dusk.

Look around...see yourself rise.

Oh, the skin, dew caressed.

Kissed by force, pulled by need, forever bound...hunger insatiable.

I'm a fighter, you are grace.

I'm percussion, you are violins.

We were an orchestra, a symphony.

No conductor, no rules

These melodies, notes of lust,

to hear them...one more time.

Ben Foxx

Undone

Hung on the hook of our blood-thirsty lust

I twist and I turn until inside out

To find the right angle

The one that you want

So you won't imply I'm not good enough

A wanton puppet I've become, a slave

It's your hands, your mouth, your approval I crave

You know all my places on an intimate basis

But so does your tongue

It finds my weak spots and tears me apart

You worship my body and rip out my heart

Just as I come completely undone

Anne Hayward

Remains

Would wanton

Moments

Find us

Where we began

That spell

Is broken now

And what remains

Is vaguely

Sweet

Cate Derham

Longing

I want to lie

In the softness

Of wildflowers

Absorb kisses from the sun

Feel love within the breeze

No longer ache

To be touched

Catherine LoFrumento

Dire

Not fate

Whim

Nor formal introduction

Romantic pairs so dire

Catch fire

And burn on instinct

SubtleHoney

Echo

Within

The chill wind

You capitulate

To stinging tears

Of rejection

We never learn

We are the echo

Infinite voids

Amplify your

Need

Kenneth Jordan

Elemental

Of tender lips,

transparent above me,

silver robe whispering

into the night air,

takes my pain

and turns it

to snow.

Ben Foxx

Burn

Taste the fire in my kiss

My dark embrace

Feel the heat of my desire

My soul in flames

Touch the heart of this inferno

And watch me burn

Karen Ohren

Embrace

Your heart whispers a soothing lullaby

A gentle cadence

Beckoning me to curl up, warm

In the memory of an embrace

Yet to be

Julie Matondi Doucet

Bookends

The first time and the last

Moments that burn behind my eyes

Bright bookends to the blurred, soft focus

Of everything that came between

How nothing else of us now is engraved in my mind

Yet carved deep into my heart

Memories remain

Quiet footnotes to our story

Written in pain

Louise Arrowsmith

Unfinished

An unfinished painting

is all that remains

for how do I fill a canvas sheet

with a ghost,

a sigh

or a pulse that no longer

beats with

mine?

George Mat

Flame

This

Dying flame

Embers sign a scar

On my naked soul

And time surely heals

Yet my neverlasting

Body aches

Still

Kenneth Jordan

A Woman

I lay aching in my bed of dreams

A woman of many skills

Lover of the darkness

Warrior of the light

Holding in my fingers

A passion, a fire

I am a keeper of the memories

I am the one that makes you weep

I walk free, untamed

I am stronger than you think

In my fragility you find desire

In my curls you find the wind

In my lips you find the secrets

In my embrace you find peace

In between my thighs you find lust

In my mind you find words

In my heart you find love

In my soul you find the woman

Me

Vlada Mars

Evening

We lie in a meadow

Languid summer heat diffuses

Drunk bees bounce off closing petals

Evening's passage begins

With coiled limbs

Roger Litherland

Inside

Each time I feel your body against his

Being brought to ecstasy

I die a little more inside

This bond between our souls

When you can't be mine

Will kill me

L. Ruben Willis

Eclipsed

Her exquisite

Now eclipsed

Under layers of

Concealment

Hiding

Tear-stains

Traced black

Into a tattoo

The brutal

Of you

Tara Fleur

Bound

Rolling deeply

into maniacal taunting.

Your eyes, staring into

my every shred of existence.

Crawling inside a curse...

resembling perfection.

Ben Foxx

Lingers

The taste of her flesh

Is a thousand miles away

Beyond introductions,

Courtship,

Pursuit

And capture

But still

It lingers on

My lips

Todd Rokholm

Two Loves

For I had loved them both

In the same season

The same moment of the same day

I had loved them both

One was my blood moon the other my morning sun

One my midnight the other daybreak

One was the fire in my belly as the other held the light

That waltzed behind my eyes

One was in my heart within the shadow of the other

For I had loved them both

And it almost killed us all

Biff Rushton

Desire's Creed

Beauty found in a glance

Trapped, spiraling down lover's trance

I held my breath, instantaneous hope

Feeling the fall down your treacherous slope

Grasping for a hand, one piece of a lifeline

Sinking further, no salvation from this decline

Swirling vortexes, emotions gone wild

Carry me to darkness, completely beguiled

Lost in your embrace, nowhere to run

Cursed with your eyes, I've come undone

Savage love, primal needs, primordial lust

Surrender brings risk, experience mistrust

Cannot fight this undying need

For passion's fire, desire's creed

Submitting now to primeval hunger

Tomorrow?

Weeping

Torn asunder

Camille Wylde

Kiss Axe

Press upon a lover's lips

Kiss to wield the axe

Cut to slit a heart in two

Who knew she might slash back

SubtleHoney

The War within Her

Front lines of love moved us forward then back

Rushed by kisses and charging arms

Faith's blaring trumpets seduced our strings of hope

We marched blindly together onto open battlefields

Holding dear to us enchanting dreams of love's conquest

Some returned heroes, others are martyred

We here are casualties with missing parts

To be counted among the dead

Shells of what we were

Not unlike body bags filled with air

Of echoing pain and a weakened pulse

Formerly ecstatic hearts

Now living out our lonely days

As ghostly epitaphs in graveyards

Dying to re-enlist

Jennifer Brown

Lost

His kisses stain my soul and purge my sin

Where fingers play on naked skin

And verses not yet penned

Bring me to the edge

And I am lost

In him

Cate Derham

Titanium

Molten eyes well

Hiding a broken soul

Deep in the depths

Tough scar tissue

Bonding the pieces

Titanium tears

Drip

Tough

Love

Roger Litherland

Once

To wake in the bleak pale of morning

Void of breath and foreseeable hope

Ill-informed of our chosen paths

As we partake in the existence of another

What more is love, than a sickness awaiting its grave?

And in the end we're left alone inside our hallowed depths

Awaiting eternal solace or perhaps a mere dark silence

Longing for warmth and life, to live again

But to love?

No, for this torturous grandeur

Claims us once

Wholly and entirely

Amarie Molina

Passion

Oh, Love!

A soft torment

Cleaving tender flesh from

Bones, melted

In passion's consuming fires

Julie Matondi Doucet

Apple-flesh

An apple picked right at the cusp, too early.

Or maybe it was rotten, sitting on the ground

in the leaves by roots weaving together

like a ball of rattlers coming out after winter.

You spit the apple's flesh in the river and watch it drown

like a witch tied down with stones.

A snake coiled around your throat,

slits for eyes, its forked tongue leaving sin kisses on your neck.

It shows its fangs, venom beaded at the tips.

And the perennials pay their last respects to the fleeting season,

The Garden of Eden.

Zak Cowell

North

There's a light, guides me through

desperate waters.

I'm a sail...and you're the wind.

Clouds bow to thee, as we slice waves.

The last bits of stardust, your pockets aglow...

The Northern Gate

Edge of night waits, as we cast off...somehow we'll make it.

By Curve of Moon...We fly.

By Splice of Stars...We run.

Nothing to stop us,

our limitations stripped, no longer bound.

Two Celestial Beings,

running through barren lands,

running with purpose,

running towards each other.

Ben Foxx

Stones

It is a winter at war

I turn stones

On silent graves

I crumble cold in dirt

Unable to remember

The last kiss goodbye

Tara Fleur

Together

Sleep with me, my love

And we'll dream together

Under the same smiling moon

Julie Matondi Doucet

Thunder

We felt the rumble

of thunder

in the storm we created

knowing it felt too right

to be wrong

and so the rain

kept falling

George Mat

Freed

Bright burning red

Cheery to see

Painful

To be

Untouch

Finally freed

Scarlet hearts

Fade to black

SubtleHoney

Your Light

In the broken hours that have no perception of light
Just a slump, where my ragged soul takes flight
I turn the hushed pages of fragmented dreams
Bound by transgressions, for what uncontrollably seems
An eternity of circles diminishing, unravelling our breath
Piece by piece, kiss by precious kiss of life beyond death
The agony of words binding our love, defying the grub of night;
I summon strength to hold you, to lead you into the light
Of the moon, of stars, of your brilliance beyond the measure
Of my humble offer, to dream of a heart I urge to treasure

Jim C. Mackintosh

Emptiness

I still ache

I still feel your fingers

Grasp tight as you tear my heart

Ripping it into raindrops

Showering my soul in the bloody sorrow

Of Yesterday's happiness

Only hoping it will grow back

Out of the inflamed emptiness

That now houses only

The echoes of my tears

Higherhawk

Solace

Too late

I am plummeting

Plunging lips kissing wild air

Tears wrenched from lids ripped

I find a drop of solace

In the submission

Roger Litherland

Almost

Part

Of you

Lives on

These rooms

Still dusted

In your magic

Flooded with

A rush of certainty

You exist

Almost tangible

Within this place

Within me

Stay here

Please

Where I can

Almost see

Your

Face

Nina Loard

Fall

Strip away the fragile surface

Pierce my tender flesh with sweet desire

Scar this waiting heart with faithless words

Tear my soul apart

And let me fall

Karen Ohren

Risen

I wish I could erase

Traces of your trespass through my heart

You've ruined me

Once I believed in you

Foolish, trusting me

I should have seen impending heartache

In your lying, loving eyes

How coyly they deceived

Beguiling me

Into a stupefied trance

Oh, how you must have delighted in your deceit

Knowing how you'd stomped the light

Out of my now ravaged heart

Much to your dismay

You'll find you left a girl

But the woman who's risen from your carnage

Won't ever be deceived again

M. B. Stephens

Asleep

Perhaps you know how you got here

reading this, awake and aware of a set beginning

Or maybe I'm dreaming you

as I am lost

somewhere asleep in the middle of these words

Susan Purr

Dormant

Lay your hands

On my skin

Resurrect my blood

Make it pound

In my dormant veins

Teach me to

Breathe

Again

Catherine LoFrumento

To Taste

Electrified

Lips touch, hips writhe

Surges swell

The mad joy

Skin on skin

Immersed within

Rise with the tides

Tasting your

Flood

Roger Litherland

Lullabye

Butterfly kisses,

Lullabye wishes.

Two fish in a barrel, delicious.

A fictitious feeling

replaced with truth.

Do I get to spin the loom?

Do I get to make it bloom?

I watch the hearts leak and the dead dreams

of lost love pool at the feet of lovers

and I collect them

like a thirsty man in the desert watches rainwater.

What do I see inside her heart?

Only silhouettes of a girl watching from a window.

Only a lotus floating, waiting to be picked.

Only a starlit sky covered with clouds

the color of a blind man's eyes.

Zak Cowell

Smokescreen

We share a cigarette

Our lips touch fleetingly on the thin sensual ream

Of tobacco

I savour your poisoned scent

Intoxicating

A connection as fragile as ash lights up my heart

The closest we'll ever get

Now I can pretend that I kissed you

Jonathan Digby

Black Violets

We wrapped ourselves
in the black violets of night
and all I could see
was the smile in her eyes
and all I could feel
was the sex on her lips
and all I could smell
was the scent of her rain
in the lightning
that struck

George Mat

Not I

I open the door

He steals in with the night

Dark in presence & desire

Kisses tumble from his lips

Tasting of whiskey

And all the promises he'll never keep

Eagerly I fill his hands

Like a marionette

His touch bringing me to life

I need him in ways that scare me

In ways he will never reciprocate

Euphoric in his embrace

I choose to ignore

The painful truth

She owns his heart

Not I

Susan Brown

My Only Chance

Look softly on me, Darling.

My shell is cracking...

and I need a tender glance.

Ben Foxx

Equal Measure

The terrifying

Deepening ache of her

To feel

To taste

To know

Her gifts surrendered

And to give

All she longs for

In equal measure

Todd Rokholm

Remember

We were drunk on one another

joyfully ripping away every concealment.

Even soft sand and waves making love to the shore

imparted no languor.

Our bodies filled with storm

murmuring lightning and thunder against wet skin.

How perfect that moment.

How beautifully devastating.

Even now your breath on my neck takes me there.

My heart remembers

everything.

Laura Lee Sweet

I Know

Sea winds shift

Blow warmer

My door creaks open

A shadow cast over

Aching floorboards

As steps draw closer

And I know

Without looking

You are here

Nina Loard

Farewell

Farewell
To late nights
Ticking off life
In the columns of a diary
Marking fake beginnings
And even faker ends
Farewell
To my darling Jacob
My dog that passed away
He was such a cool cuddle
And my very best'est ever friend
Farewell
To not listening to my heart
Wasting kisses
Smiles
And energy
On the easy to arrive
Then, even easier to depart
Farewell
To searching
For what I truly do not need
Like empty ambitions
Lusty longings
And belongings to a world
Packed plastic with envy and greed

Farewell

To a cupboard

Stuffed with clothes

I no longer wear

I'm giving them away

To a shivering lady, look

She sat hungry over there

Farewell

To the people

Who didn't really care

And farewell to those I trusted

So impolite

So selfish

And so never, ever there

Farewell

To a zillion poems

Given a new life outside my mind

Forward, forward, forward

No point ever in rewind

Farewell

To strangers

I gave what little I have in kind

Farewell

To holes in pockets

Where I lost all sense of self

Farewell

To dust collecting

Layers of old, dead lovers' skins

I now blow off

With vigor from my solid cranial shelf

Farewell

To another year in a life

Not so ordinary, but extraordinary!

Farewell

To pointless worries

A cross of callous contraries

Farewell

To forgetting

Always keep forgetting

I'm not afraid of being alone

For we are all travelling as one

Are not we?

Farewell

For not fare-welling:

No never, never fare-welling

Because I am

Yes truly, I am greeting

Not being one of the clones

For these are My New Years

So, say hello

Without unnecessary fears

For I am nothing so special

But I am me, yes me

A Woman of Bones

Tara Fleur

One More Break

You speak to me of the sensual

Defrosting the chill

From my cold, nearly dead heart

Now open, bared, vulnerable

Then you freeze with your fears

I'm scared too, now more than ever

Are you going to stay and complete what you started?

Or will you walk away

And leave me drowning in a scarlet river

From a heart that couldn't afford

One more break?

Janie Gouge

Threads

We are the players and the audience

In our trunk show

We measure twice

Cut once

And stitch each other

Back together

In love's threads

Jeffrey M. Kirn

Forbidden Rainbows

Why is there still such a thing as forbidden love?

Somehow shamed, denied its chosen caress

A heart bound, locked in a chest without a key

Love for another safe, beyond the scrawny cove of scrutiny

Judgmental ravens demand to confess

Possession of a rainbow, unfurled and free

Draped on the shoulders by sweet Liberty

Its ribbons of freedom, a passionate embrace

Ignoring the walls of crumbling spite

Damn the spume of that ragged trinity

Timendi cause est nescire - declared with grace,

Ignorance is the cause of fear - walk into the light

Untie your bonds and let the rainbow soar

Beyond Forbidden's walls - a heart tethered no more

Jim C. Mackintosh

Shiver

You slip

From my arms

The taste of your kiss

Still on my lips

A shiver of longing upon cooling skin

The ache of loss relived

As the memory of your touch begins to fade

And dawn steals your shadow from the room

Karen Ohren

Aftertaste

Do you hear the echo from my soul

It cries out in hope of reaching the light I once held close

Yet the ache you left behind weakens my plea

It steals the strength of my courage

To spread my wings and fly free

Feeding my fear drops of false hope

That dance on the tip of my tongue

Numbing my heart and leaving

The bitter aftertaste

Of you

Higherhawk

True

Voice something other

Than words to me

My mind has grown tired

Of language

Voice something

Strangely beautiful

We'll call it

True

Okiethyme

With

My fate,

to find you.

Once again

dragging chains,

self-built.

Denied entrance

to The Gates...

I've broken into gates before,

I need you first.

Ben Foxx

Melancholy

I know when that melancholy approaches.

You continually look past me

as if the next form holds the woman of your dreams.

My heart weeps even though I love you

with the understanding of a like mind.

Write that poem to me that you are composing in your soul.

I have loved you, worshipped you, trailed after your every song.

I deserve to be the one who will calm your storm

and be a safe harbor

for all your deepest

adoration.

Laura Lee Sweet

Dead Dust

We burned so brightly

Dimming far-flung suns

Love and desire entwined

In passion's pulse

With one final upheaval

We exploded

Scattering galaxies

Like a handful

Of dead dust

R. M. Worley

Of Mountains

Granite can break, easily enough

From the weight of hearts falling in love

Fissures form on mountaintops

Letting light in before getting lost

In the depths of cascading passions

Flowing downhill

And pooling low on the bedrock

Mountains have been moved

Have risen from the deepest seas unfathomed

In a rivalry between Gaia's love of the world

And Eros' world of love

In the dirt and stone

In boulders washed from the mound

There rests the strength found in love

Solid and abounding

Woven by the gods into the soil that nurtures our food

And in turn, our souls

Kevin Hulit

Faded

I close my eyes

To taste your kiss

The breathless touch of memory

The sweet surrender of my soul

A faded hope

My heart cannot

Resist

Karen Ohren

The Geese Carry Her Love Away

The sun that hangs in the sky, she said,

Will sink beneath the trees

And darkness fall on the green earth

While the leaves sigh in the breeze.

All that lives will pass, she said,

As sure as night follows day,

But I will love you still, she said,

Though the sun will fade away.

Though the moon forget to rise, she said,

And the swallow bring back the spring,

I will love you more than you'll ever know,

For you're gone with the geese on the wing.

Jane Dougherty

Stillness

In the stillness
Her goodbye remains
Our pulse a promise on the breeze
Turned tinnitus in ringing seizure
Sharp within yearning veins
Take this beating flesh
So sweet the caramelizing core
Dripping into my lungs
Stealing my sugary breath so fresh

I want –
I want it to stop

Her wake, her pricking scent
All pain in echoing chambers
Where love once bloomed, then withered
Like its life was spent in vain
In the stillness it quakes
Powerless to a rhythm
In memory's sun-kissed drop
In this sadness I shake
And so it must stop

Jeffrey M. Kirn

Then...

To never know the feeling,

of sweet, soft torment,

without the absence

of your flesh,

stolen from me,

every second you're away.

Ben Foxx

Lilith

She’s a full hotel,

the "No Vacancy" sign off,

the closed restaurant with the lights on.

Jezebel: the guitar always without a string.

Out to consume since the moment she left the womb.

You’ll pay the price with a smile of broken teeth

as she feasts on your convenience,

on hearts that stand like soldiers at attention,

wasting borrowed time and bodies.

She won’t take no for an answer, but you will, just you watch.

You won’t know it ‘til the world is ending,

and it’s all your fault.

A forbidden fruit that never ripens,

barely hanging out of reach.

Zak Cowell

Discontent

I always ran away from you

In the way you touched my soul

I'd never felt my heart beat the way it did

When you were near or afar

It may have scared me

So, when it was the mind that led the heart

There was no heart to grow

And when I reminisce I sit in deep lament

Screaming at my demons' seasons of discontent

I hope my heart one day will tell my mind to calm

To feel your face once more in my aching palm

George Mat

Earth-spin

In the second it took

For me to know

My eyes could never

See another

The earth-spin paused

What seemed a year

As my future danced

Before me

Okiethyme

Revealed

How many crass words can I use to reveal my longing?
You are all sweet strength and tender manhood.
At the sound of your voice my heart beats my whole body.
This conflagration will destroy all but the one who truly deserves it.
You are that man.
If I touch you here, will you press your length against my hand?
If I kiss you there, will you moan my name?
I can no longer withhold the truth from myself
but I will continue to hide each throbbing ache,
smile at your face,
and imagine the smell of you
on my body.

Laura Lee Sweet

Space & Time

If you travel fast enough

Time will pause

I desired to reach that point

I desired to breach the possibilities

Of my own existence

I reached out to the limits of my universe

I stretched the underlying knowledge

To its brink

I discovered and I explored

Past the stars and planets

Through asteroid belts and comet tails

Into the void of dark matter

I came and you conquered my heart

For inside your heart

I managed to travel fast enough

To make time stop

I found the ends of my universe

Resided in yours

Timmy Fenning

Lust

Flashed & flushed

With fleshy lust

Soul afire

Eager

Blistering

Raging forever

Endeavoring to devour

Showering love & forgiveness

Roger Litherland

Carousel

Exquisite, the pain

Pricking the memory

Of what once

Was a waking dream

No beginning and

No ending

A carousel of hopes

Spun out of

Nothing

R. M. Worley

Disposable

The world is of course

Your oyster

To judge

Pick and pluck

A condescending look

A patronizing glance

Another disposable romance

Roger Litherland

Scattered

Drowning

In discarded affections

Suffocating in disappointments

No air

No breathing

Heart barely beating

If I wake into darkness

Know you put me there

That is what I leave you

Suffer

For I have suffered

Hurting while you sleep

Breaking while you laugh

The stars I wished on

Have all burned out

No more light

No more wishes

Everything that never was

Is scattered to the wind

K. M. Bedolla

Broken Beauty

Gathering up

What's left of fantasy

She holds the brokenness

Bare hands cradle crystal shards

SubtleHoney

Our Show

Never a tearless year I've known

Never a tearless year I'll see

My months and days

Come and go

Like tides through the hours

I'm showered with love

From every age of family & friend

Stories begin where others end

I bow to rituals of my time

And when I find myself

Amongst a tribe, I dance accordingly

My determination set only to round

Each bend of this river in which I swim

This winding river of breath

Bordered by birth, by death

The borders I see encountered

Each day by my life's companions

The borders of hello and farewell

That seem illusory as smoke

A newborn child in my arms

Looks up at me and in her eyes

I see the life of all who have gone before

And all who will ever be

She, an infant instant

Of our collective story

Her warm, sweet breath

Assures the drama

Of days, months and years

Is merely a play

And I am transported

Beyond the stage, over the rafters

And through the cosmos

By one tiny form

By holding one life...any life....I let go

And dissolve into the mystery

Of our show

Okiethyme

Two Thieves

We both know how this ends

And finally acceptance denial, jealousy, spite

Replaced with understanding

Acknowledgement of our fate

Six years and we've become

Stolen moments

Secret places

Erased texts

Blocked calls

Not tomorrow, he's off

Not today, she's home

I miss you

I need you

The taste of you

The feel of you

My heart broke when you didn't call

Don't ever leave me alone

No one but you

One day when the kids are older

Forever my love

I will love you forever

So, we stay within this dance

Knowing one day the sun will fall from the sky

And burn through our forever

But, until then we will pine away

Steal what we can

Two thieves swallowed by the red of our hearts

Biff Rushton

Downpour

Unable to feel
in the desolate terrain
of two hearts
as my flesh folds within hers
and emerald eyes
mesmerized
in the
downpour

George Mat

Dandelion

Dreaming

In downy

Splendor

Atop the

Warm breath

Of summer

Heart pounding

Before a kiss

Aching to be

The wish

Blown

From your

Lips

Nina Loard

Voice Swells

I sail on

The rise & fall

Of your voice

On the swells

Of your phrasing

I kiss the words

That fly from your lips

Like lovebirds

Okiethyme

Wanderlust

A pick

An insatiable want

I throw a bone

To my cold and broken

Wanderlust

Where falling

Through the ice

Feels like love

Jeffrey M. Kirn

Between Words

I don't know

When no word from you

Is n-o

When it is

K-n-o-w

Either way chips into walls of days

Even Jericho fell. Babylon. The Maginot line.

Even a heart cracks

Its pieces fall away

Always in all ways

A way

A why

A because

For which we even knowing remain unprepared

Our bodies unbraced

Even time runs out as clear before our eyes

As stillness

In a bottom heavy glass

Pulls us down

Jonathan Yungkans

In the Back

For you

You in the back

Hiding behind

The lies you were told

The scornful voices

Unheard in the noise

For your heart

I write

Jeffrey M. Kirn

Separated

Palpable

The feelings of those

With no means of contact

With no love for themselves

Unforgiving

Are the lives of those

Led by the love of more

Unaware, unable to sever the hold

Another hole, another sorrow

Another grows cold

If only as a means of escape

Bleeding days

Breaking beneath the weight

The waiting, the waste

Seeking relief until there's nothing left

No love for a life

Laced with unease and regret

Self-abandoned, addicted

Left alone with the vacuum created

With the ache of being

No longer our own

Without love

Separated

Jake Corr

Past Caring

I rode the ache of it

Into the absence

Where my impoverishment

Could be chilled to numbness

A day can be carried on

Legs can lift and feet placed

When the grit and rough landings

Are no longer of mind

Built, spurted, spent

Love's quick descent

Naught but stained sheets

Where two flaccid hearts

Continued to beat

Way past

Caring

Todd Rokholm

Unkind

You picked me up

On a hot summer's day

And led me down

A path of lust and love

But then one day

You threw me away

Leaving me shredded and bleeding

In the arch of my own despair

A reeling feeling

This abandonment unkind

A sick little game

Being plied with words

Only to destroy me

With your beautiful

Verse

Suzanne Caldwell

Insatiable

We speak of it with such fickleness

All good flowing from fingertips

And nothing but lies spewed from bitter lips

We speak as if we comprehend

The nature of this particular beast

A hungry insatiable fellow

Who grinds bones

With jagged

Teeth

Melissa Walker

Want

I want

The kind of love

That warmth

Of a fireplace at night

The freshness

Of first snowfall

The pulse

Of a rushing waterfall

That love

A. M.

Another

This is but a life

A swirling, failing grasp

At catching you

Our fingers brushed

As we danced

But I could not grab hold

I await another

Todd Rokholm

Circle

Petal of wound

Flower that blossoms when

You touch

The last dormant

Promise

Of love cold and broken

Where pain's

Circle begins

Jonathan Yungkans

Genesis

As I cannot

Recall the moment

Of my conception

So, too, your

Inconceivable

Presence in me

You breathe

And my cells are

Enlivened

Okiethyme

Fantasies on Fire

Fantasies catch like fire

A rush of white hot desire

Until my brain cells spark

Stars in the depths of my dark

These epic loves are easy to dream

A perfect illusion

To snuff out the scream

Of realities suffocating grip

For real love can

Shatter and rip

Ashley Marie Egan

Faint Glow

Where shall eternity lay

if not in celestial light?

A faint glow

as she dances in moonlight

the moment I close my eyes

and wish

George Mat

Broken Heart

Broken heart
Stands at shore's edge
Weeping as lovers kiss
Losing the battle in each crashing wave
Broken heart
Listens ever so quietly
Leaping as you say her name
Taking the memory to bed nightly
Broken heart
Lost in the crowd
Takes tea at a side table
Emotions set to observe
Broken heart
Over dinner with friends
Laughs a little too heartily
As glasses clink & toasts are made
Broken heart
Cradles a child, hiding the ache
Holding oh so tightly & hurrying away
Broken heart
Chats via phone weekly
With friends & family
All too often heard to exclaim
'Yes, I'm okay. Thank you'

Nina Valentin

Entombed

What weathered stone

The whip and chill

Of her breaking churn

Has left me

Smooth, cold and still

As a corpse entombed

And content to lie

Todd Rokholm

Closure

And

Now I must

Remember to forget

SubtleHoney

###

THE WRITERS

Louise Arrowsmith – DeepInkyBlue@deepinkyblue

K. M. Bedolla – K.M. Bedolla@WriteR_Wr0ng

Jennifer Brown – Gaia Eden@SHEIKHGALERIE

Susan Brown – Misty Grey@MissTgrey

Suzanne Caldwell – Suzanne@MRIGal3

Jake Corr – http://www.breakingthewinds.com

Zak Cowell

Cate Derham – Cate Derham@Cate_Derham

Jonathan Digby – Jonathan Digby@JonDigbyAuthor

Julie Matondi Doucet – Julie Anne@JulieforBoston

Jane Dougherty – Jane Dougherty@MJDougherty33

Carol Drummond – Carol@CarolDrummond4

Ashley Marie Egan – Ashley Marie Egan@DarlingAshes

John Feaster

Timmy Fenning – Timmy Fenning@PoemsAndBowTies

Tara Fleur – Woman of Bones@TaraFleurs

Ben Foxx – Ben@WillyGCmas

Janie Gouge – Heartsong@LoveCallsYou

Anne Hayward – Persephone@wordcra7y

Higherhawk – Higherhawk@Higherhawk

Kevin Hulit – Kevin Hulit@kevinhulit

Kenneth Jordan

Jeffrey M. Kirn

Roger Litherland – Arthur Sleep@ThePoetryThumb

Nina Loard – Nina@SkyeTrilogy

Catherine LoFrumento – Catherine@Catherin03

A. M. – i AM@_chapter_3

Jim C. Mackintosh – JimCMackintosh@JimCMackintosh

Vlada Mars – Vlada Mars@VladaMars

George Mat

Amarie Molina – Amarie Molina@AuthorAmarie

Karen Ohren – Karen Ohren@KarenOhren

Okiethyme – Okiethyme@Okiethyme

Susan Purr – Susan Purr@SusanPurr

Jacquie Roberts – Entirety@Entiretyinbits

Todd Rokholm – Todd Rokholm@MyPrompts

Elsie Rose – Elsie Rose@somewhereaclock

Biff Rushton – Tx_SolblueSol@Vudu_poet

M. B. Stephens – Marla's Musings@mnm67

SubtleHoney – SubtleHoney™@SubtleHoney

Laura Lee Sweet

Nina Valentin – Lady Bird@_iLadyBird

Melissa Walker – M@queenbukowski

L. Ruben Willis – Tortured Cyclone@TorturdCyclone

Bambie Wodkins – Bambie Wodkins@BambieWodkins

R. M. Worley – Lady of the Storms@MadQueenStorm

Camille Wylde – Camille R. Wylde@CamWylde

Jonathan Yungkans – Jonathan Yungkans@JonYungkans

THE COLLECTION

Who am I to think I can create a poetry collection?

Such an excellent question and one I considered a few times before deciding to press forward. It came down to an easy answer. I've always loved poetry. The first writing I secretly penned in my flower-covered journal was poetry.

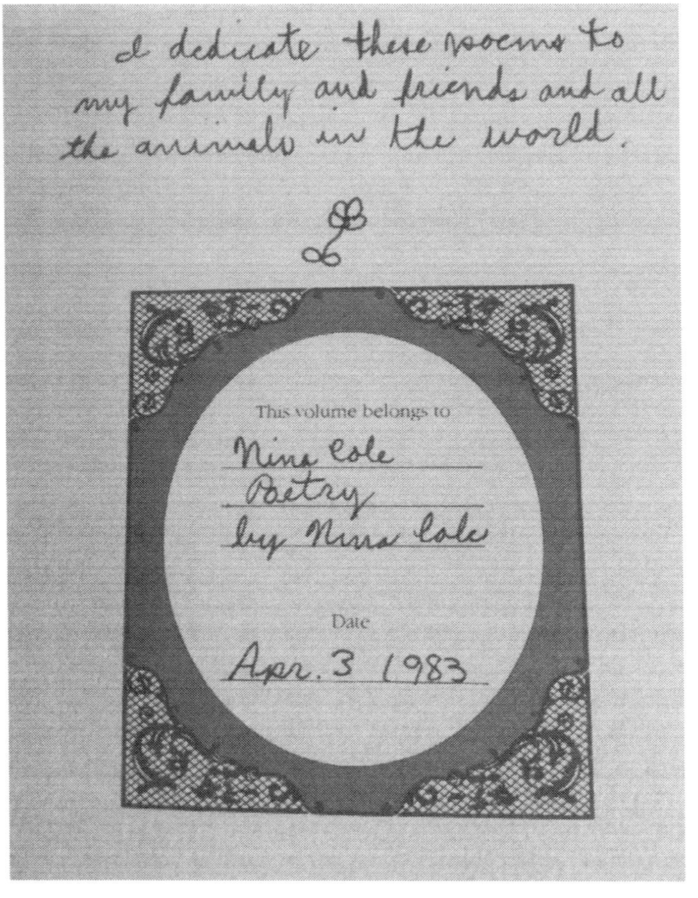

And, when you find the poems you love, the way they build up and break you – it makes you hungry for more.

It comes as no surprise that I became a writer and then started to compose poetry on Twitter, eventually forming my own site to share the work of others.

@FieryVerse began in June 2014, at the urging of my editor and writing coach, T. R. Perri - @TRPerri. By publication of this collection, I will have commented on and shared poetry over 100,000 times. Though I am sure some out there have read more poetry than I have in the last six months, I doubt there are many.

Fiery Verse is a unique story in that it has grown into a publishing venture, but it started as just one of many writing challenges featured in social media. I've taken this opportunity to list a few resources below for writers who are interested in taking part.

Thank you for the support of this collection, these writers and for helping to keep the art of poetry alive.

Micropoetry Society@pssms
http://www.micropoetry.com

THE WRITE LIST@thewritelist
http://www.thewritelist.wordpress.com

Prompt Attention@PromptAttn

PROMPTS@SemperSum
http://www.sempersum.wordpress.com

39241736R00107

Made in the USA
Lexington, KY
13 February 2015

MARVEL
www.marvel.com

Panini BOOKS

Spider-Man and Friends™ 2009 Annual is published by Panini Publishing, a division of Panini UK Ltd. Mike Riddell, Managing Director. Alan O'Keefe, Managing Editor. Mark Irvine, Production Manager. Office of publication: Panini UK Ltd., Brockbourne House, Mount Ephraim, Tunbridge Wells, Kent TN4 8BS.

£6.99

MARVEL
SPIDER-MAN
& Friends
Welcome, gang! Turn the pages to read about some of our most amazing adventures!
And whilst you're at it, check out some of the cool puzzles and things to to do!
30

47

36

6

King of the Sandcastle

Communication

Nearly there!
Hulk digs!
After a long time and a lot of hard work, the sandcastle is looking really good!
We've finished!
THWIPP!
Spidey places a flag atop the highest part of Castle Marvel.
The Hulk collects sea water in his HUGE hands to trap some sea water for the moat.

Oh no!
But the water disappears into the sand! The Hulk can't fill the moat quickly enough!
Huh!
The moat is too big! "We'll never be able to fill it!" cries the Hulk. But Captain America suggests using his shield as a bowl to bring more water to the moat.
It's raining!
But Storm has a better idea! She uses her powers to create a special rain shower.

Waahhhh!
Oh no! The rain is too much and the moat overflows before Storm can stop it. The sand turns to mud beneath their feet. Yuck!
The rain is so heavy it flattens the sandcastle. Captain America uses his shield to protect his friends from the downpour.
But it's too late for the super sandcastle and the sand washes away. But the friends have had great fun... and the next sand castle will be bigger than ever!
The End

Who's Who?

Creativity

Spider-Man's friends all have special powers.
But what can each of them do?

Spider-Man

Spidey can climb walls, has superhuman strength and a sixth sense that warns him of danger!

Hulk

The Hulk likes to jump, lift heavy things and if he gets hurt, can heal his wounds really quickly!!

Costume Capers!

Every Super Hero needs a costume!

So do you think you can work out who's costume belongs to whom, just by matching up the colours? Draw a line from the description to the hero...

My colours are green and purple!

Hey! Mine's blue and yellow.

My costume is red, blue and white!

My costume is red and blue.

Can you colour these circles with the correct colour?

red green blue yellow

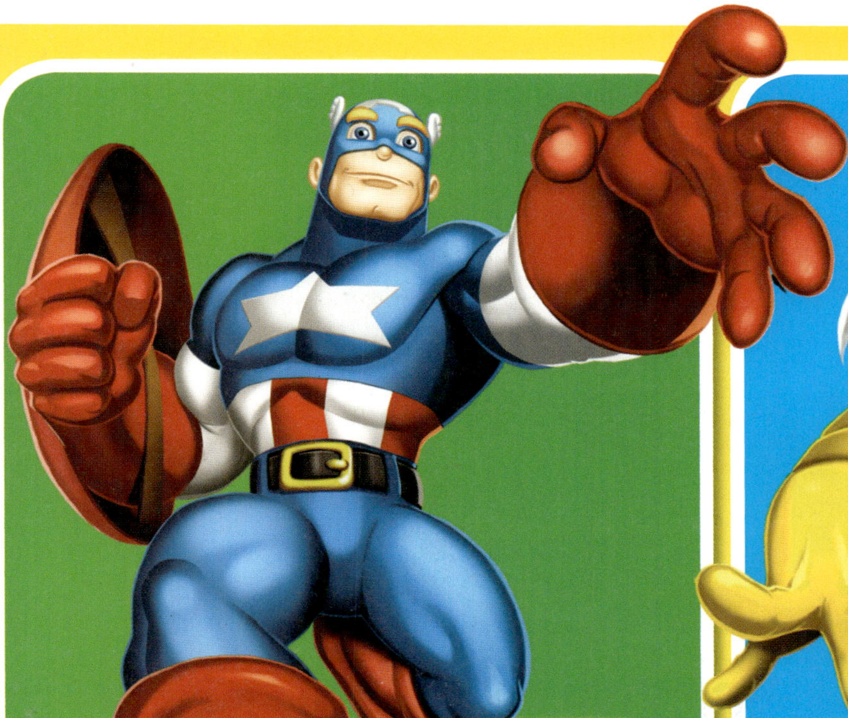

Captain America

Captain America is a super-athlete, who can do pretty much everything really well!

Storm

She can control the weather, creating rain, lightning or even snow!

What's your super-power?

Can you jump high? Run fast? Or perhaps you've got a special move (like, a super-handstand!)

Write your super-power in the box below

My Super-Power is:

Jumping HiGH

Colour the tick when you have finished

Adventure at the Zoo

Story: Rik Hoskin Art: Nigel Dobbyn

Spidey finds that the 'cat' caught in the tree is more than he bargained for... it's a lion cub, part of the family of "big cats". It would be dangerous to enter the lion enclosure, even if it was to help!

The zookeeper tells Spidey that the lion cub climbed into the tree alone but got confused, and is too scared to come down!

Spidey tells the zookeeper that he can get to the cub without disturbing the grown-ups. "At least, I hope I can," he adds.

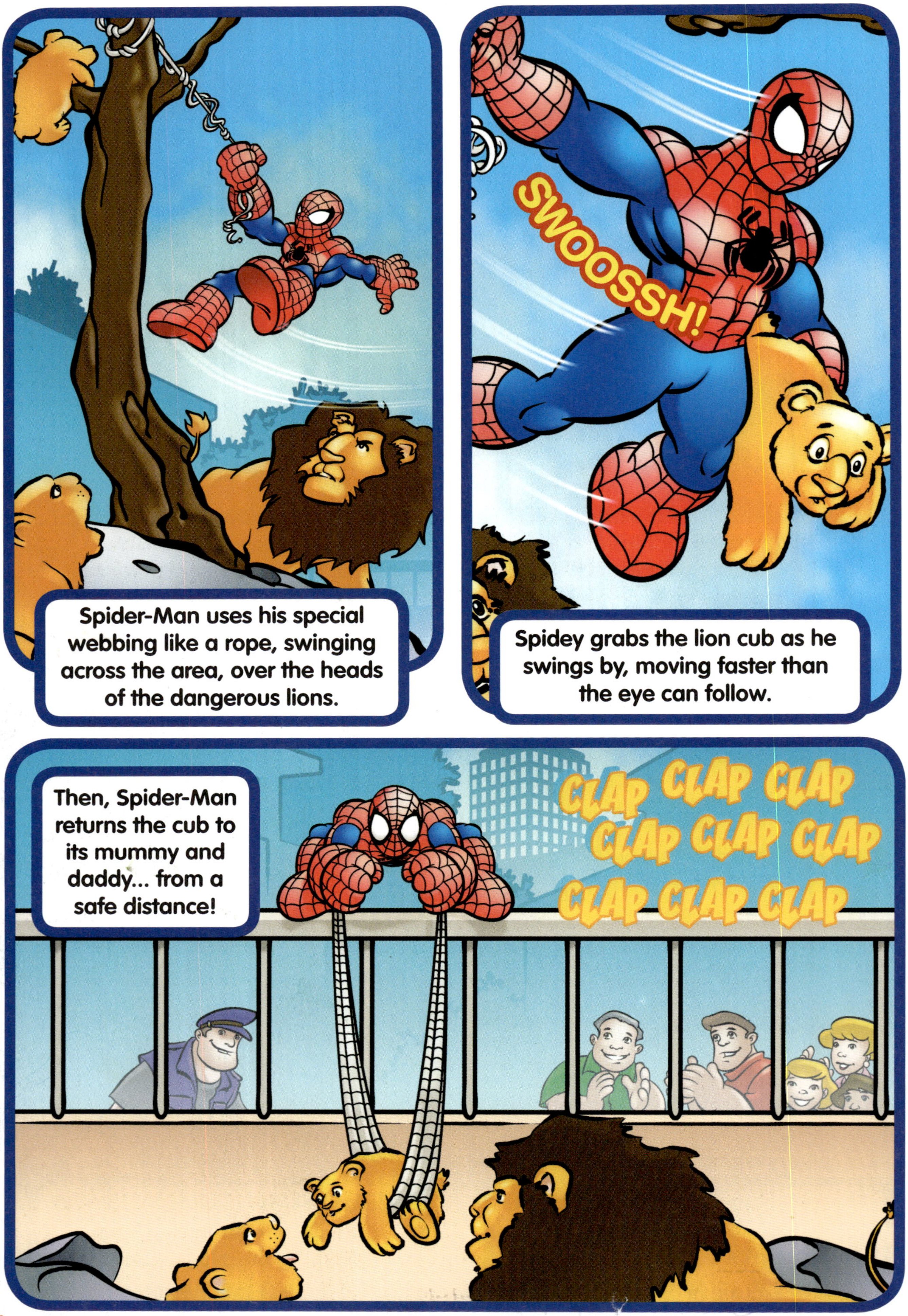
Spider-Man uses his special webbing like a rope, swinging across the area, over the heads of the dangerous lions.
SWOOSSH!
Spidey grabs the lion cub as he swings by, moving faster than the eye can follow.
Then, Spider-Man returns the cub to its mummy and daddy... from a safe distance!
CLAP CLAP CLAP
CLAP CLAP CLAP
CLAP CLAP CLAP

The zookeeper thanks Spidey with a special gift... free entry to the zoo for the hero and his friends! "But where have my pals gone?" says Spidey.

Spidey rushes through the crowd, guided by his spider-sense, as he tries to find his friends. Spidey thinks he knows where he will find Lizard...

Did you guess? Spidey finds them in... THE REPTILE HOUSE! Spidey says they can use the free tickets next Saturday. Lizard likes the sound of that... he wants to watch the lizards in the reptile house again!

The End

Who's Who?

Observation

Spider-Man's friends all have special powers. But what can each of them do?

Doctor Octopus

Doc Ock just loves science - especially inventing new things! And his extra arms come in handy!

Lizard

Our green-skinned friend is really brainy! He also has the muscles to match!

Cyclops

Cyclops always wears his special red glasses and can fire powerful beams from them!

Spider-Girl

She can climb walls, has super-strength and can shoot webbing - just like Spidey!

Animal instinct

All of the super heroes on this page get their powers from animals... apart from one. Who is it?

Match up the silhouette of each animal to the super hero and see who's left!

Wolverine

He has a great sense of smell, is super-strong and can heal himself if he gets hurt!

Wolf

Octopus

Spider

Lizard

Which animal would YOU be?

If you could have the super powers of any animal, which would it be? Maybe you'd like to fly high like an eagle, or swim like a fish?

Write your favourite animal here, in the box:

My favourite animal is:

BIG BIRD (spider man) ....

Colour the star if you got all the questions right!

Let's Play Catch!

Communication

Story: Rik Hoskin Art: Nigel Dobbyn

Spider-Man can't resist having some fun. Wolverine's keen senses mean he never loses track of the shield.
Thor is so strong he can throw it much further than the others...
Uh-oh!
... but his aim isn't very good! The shield gets stuck in a tree.

They cannot decide who should get the shield back.
Captain America says they could make a competition of it - to see who can climb the tree the quickest!
Verily, I should have flown!
Thor may be the strongest, but his cape isn't very good for climbing trees!
SNIKT
Wolverine's claws are really useful for climbing. He keeps up with Spider-Man almost the whole way up the trunk.

But Spidey is the best at climbing, just like a real spider. He reaches the top of the tree before the others...

... but not before Spider-Girl, who's been here all along! "You're so slow at climbing," she laughs.

Spider-Man disagrees! "Race you to the bottom!" he tells her, and off they go again.

The End

All about...

SPIDER-MAN

Observation

Spider-Man can climb walls, has superhuman strength and a sixth sense that warns him of danger!

He can also shoot webbing, just like a real spider!

How many spider-symbols has Spider-Man left on the page?

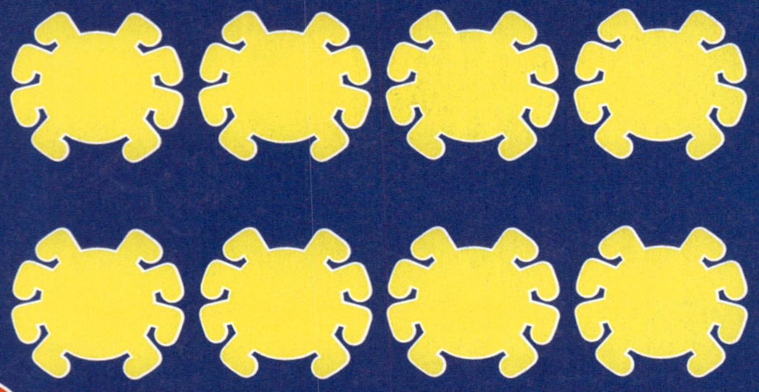

Draw a circle around the right answer.

6 7 8

How many times can you see the word **spider** in the word search? Circle the word **spider** each time you see it.

s	p	i	d	e	r	m
p	k	t	f	b	a	n
i	s	p	i	d	e	r
d	i	d	w	x	y	o
e	a	v	m	q	s	p
r	s	p	i	d	e	r
f	e	s	v	h	o	m

The first one is done for you!

How many times did the word appear? Circle the right answer.

2 3

4 5

Which web leads to Spider-Man? Is it a, b or c?

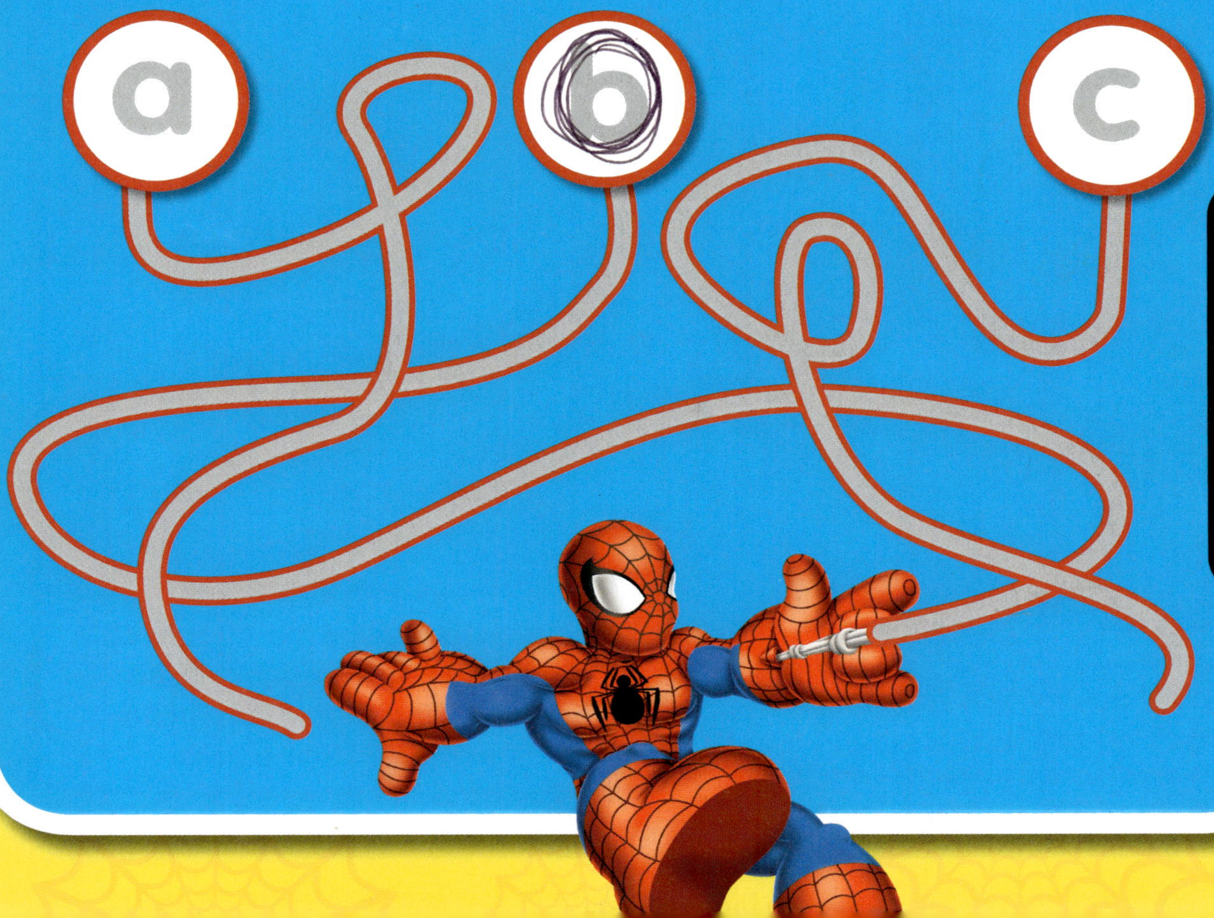

Colour the star if you finished everything on the page!

The Great Big Big Foot Hunt

Story: Rik Hoskin Art: Nigel Dobbyn

Wolverine explains that the Abominable Snowman is a giant monster rumoured to live in the mountains.
It is also known as the Yeti, Sasquatch and Big Foot--because of the large footprints it leaves.
"How do we find it?" Rhino asks. Wolverine's super sense of smell has already picked up its scent.
"It's right behind us," Wolverine tells his friends. "Everyone get ready."

Suddenly, the monster comes crashing through the trees.
CRASH!
Although he's scared, the Rhino doesn't run away.
Charge!
CRASH!
The Rhino's special power is his ability to charge at things, knocking them down---just like a real rhinoceros.
Bleaghh! Stinky!
The Rhino wins, but not before getting a face full of Big Foot's big foot!
THWIPP!
Hidden in the trees above, Spider-Man drops his webbing on the Abominable Snowman.

We're the best!
Spider-Man and his friends are relieved. Big Foot won't be menacing the campsite again.
No1
Spidey gets first prize for netting the catch of the day!
The End

Who's talking?

Spider-Man and his friends love to talk whilst exploring the mountains. But who is saying what?!

Draw a line from each speech balloon to the right person...

Abominable Snowman

Colour the star if you have finished!

Count on it!

The Abominable Snowman has been stomping around this page with his big hairy feet! How many steps has he taken?

Write your answer here:

steps

The Abominable Snowman isn't the only person with big feet! Who else runs around without any shoes on? Colour the right head to answer the question!

Beast's Story Time

The Dog Washer

Communication

Story: Rik Hoskin Art: Nigel Dobbyn

Finding out where all the water went sounds like super hero work.

LET'S FOLLOW IT!
Spider-Girl soon finds a strange hose. Maybe this has something to do with the empty pool.

The heroes are very careful when they follow the hose. They don't want to slip on the wet floor around them.

YIP!
SPLISH-SPLASH!
It's Doctor Octopus! He loves building new machines.
IT'S A DOG WASH!
Doctor Octopus tells them his latest invention could clean all the dogs in the neighbourhood in a few hours.
"But you took all the pool water," Spidey says. "Where are the kids supposed to swim?"

HEY!
Doc Ock is telling them how much more important his invention is than a swimming pool. But his first customer doesn't agree!
"Dogs don't like being washed by machines the way cars do," Doctor Octopus says as they put everything back.
The dog may not like Doc Ock's machine, but it sure loves playing in the pool!
The End

A splash

Creativity

# of colour!

Spider-Man, Doctor Octopus and Spider-Girl need some colour! Think you can help?

Colour Guide

Spider-Man

Doctor Octopus

Spider-Girl

Colour the star when you have finished

Farm Fix-Up!

Story: Rik Hoskin Art: Nigel Dobbyn

It is a very windy evening. Spider-Man can barely swing in a straight line.

"I think I'd better walk home," Spidey decides after being blown off course for the third time.

The next day, Spider-Man sees three sheep walking past his house. "Escaped sheep must be Super Hero work!" Spidey says.

Spidey and his friends go to investigate. When they reach the local farm, they find it is a mess.
The farmer explains that the strong winds blew his fences over--all of his farm animals have escaped.
STAY!
BAA?
The heroes say that they will save all of the animals. Thor uses his big hammer to rebuild the fences.

Cyclops uses his special eye-beam to make a deep ditch that the cows cannot cross to escape.
QUACK!
THWIP!
THWIP!
Spidey and the Silver Surfer combine their super powers to catch some chickens. The Surfer uses his big surfboard as a barricade.
WOOF!
The farmer helps, too. He has a specially trained dog who can make the geese go back to their home.

It takes a lot of work, but finally all the animals are returned to their rightful places at the farm.
WHO'S HUNGRY?
The farmer is very pleased with the super friends. His wife says that they deserve a super meal.
They all eat yummy eggs from the chickens and drink glasses of fresh milk from the cows... perfect food for Super Heroes!
The End

Can you

It has been a really windy day at the farm! Can you help make sure all of the animals are safe? Let's do some counting!

see?

Observation

How many cows can you count?

2 3 4 5 6

How many chickens can you see?

2 3 4 5 6

How many white chickens are there?

1 2 3 4 5

How many brown cows can you see?

1 2 3 4 5

Colour the star if you answered all the questions!

Is It Home Time?

Communication

Story: Rik Hoskin Art: Nigel Dobbyn

It's the end of the day at Spider-Man's school. The teacher is reading a super story to the class about a scary giant. Everyone enjoys story time.

Today, the story seems to be going on forever. The Lizard raises his hand so that he can ask a question. "Can we go home yet?" he asks.

It is past home time. "We should have heard the last bell by now," the teacher says. Spider-Man thinks that something strange is going on.

The teacher decides that they should all look for the missing bell. It could be anywhere in the school.

The Hulk can easily lift a desk over his head, so he helps Cyclops search their classroom. But they don't find the bell.

SNIFF
Wolverine and Thor search the school canteen. They find lots of funny tastes and smells, but they don't find the bell.

It is lots of fun searching the playground-everyone wants to join in! But, they don't find the bell there, either.

The heroes cannot find the bell in the school library either. But they do find lots of exciting books about pirates and dinosaurs and Vikings.

"We've looked everywhere," Spider-Man tells his teacher. "Are you sure?" she asks Spidey.

PRINCIPAL
Spidey remembers the one place they haven't looked--the Principal's office. The Principal is the most important teacher at the school.
The Principal shows Spider-Man that the bell has broken. He can't make it ring. Spidey has an idea.
DING
DING
Spider-Man uses his sticky webbing to fix the school bell. Then he rings it, so that everyone knows it is time to go home.
The End

Observation

Ring the bell!

Can you help Spider-Man and Hulk find the school bell? Draw a line through the maze to get to it.

The Beast is Blue

Communication

Story: Rik Hoskin Art: Nigel Dobbyn

COOL!
The Beast has been doing some special experiments. He shows Spider-Man all the strange things he's been working on.
SNAP!
"This is my special experiment!" the Beast tells Spidey. Inside is a room full of strange plants. They are blue and furry, just like the Beast.
OH BOY!
The Beast plans to use his plants to find a cure for his blue fur but it looks like the mutant plants have ideas of their own!

SNAP!
"Your plants are out of control!" Spidey says. The heroes will have to stop them before they get loose and cause trouble all over town.
YOU'RE COMPOST, BUB!
Wolverine uses his special claws like a cat to prune the plants, but he cannot reach them all. Spider-Man's web can't stop them all either.
The mutant plants soon escape the greenhouse. "We have to stop them," Spidey tells his friends.

"Use your lightning powers," Spidey tells Storm. Storm agrees, even though she doesn't like to hurt plants.
KRAKOOM!
There is a loud boom of thunder and a bright bolt of lightning bursts from the clouds at Storm's command, zapping the strange plants.
The BEAST HOUSE
The threat is over. "I don't know why you want to get rid of your blue fur," Spidey tells the Beast.
Storm agrees. "We love you just the way you are," she says.
The End

Spot the difference!

Observation

Spidey and the gang are having a secret meeting at their Treehouse. Can you find 5 differences between these two pictures?

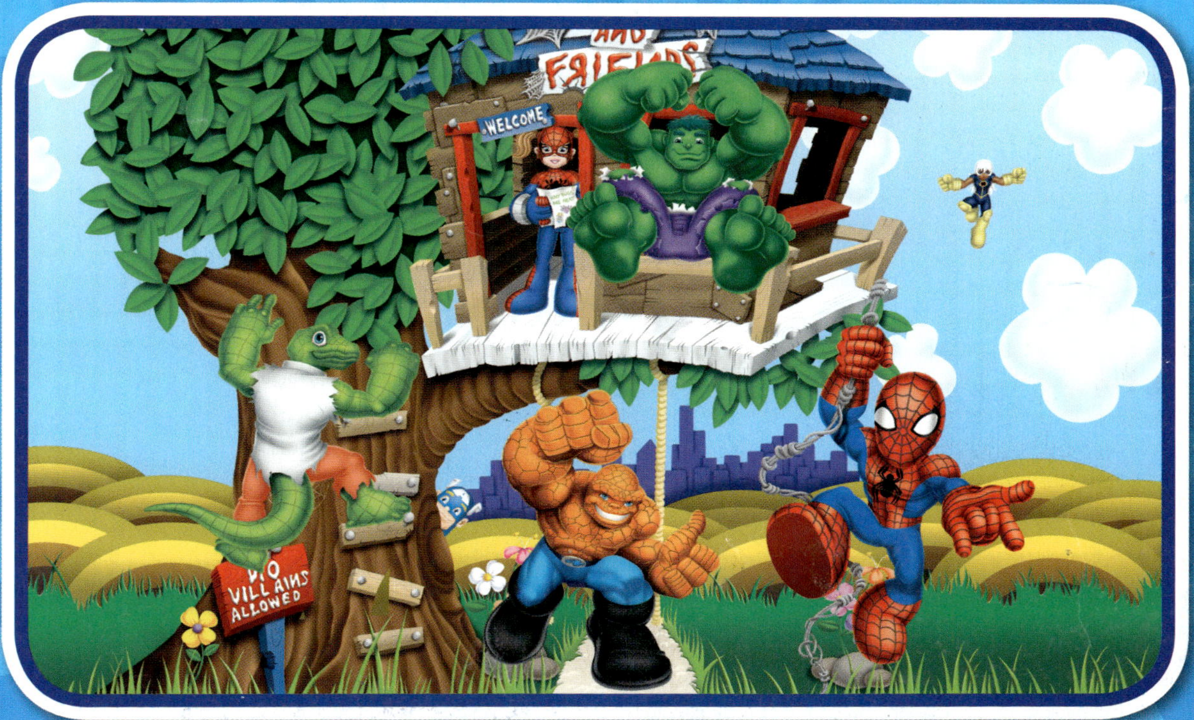

Answers: Lizard's shorts, Spider-Girl in tree house, Spidey's head, Captin America behind the tree, Storm is smaller.

Telling the time!

Can you help Spider-Man find out what time it is? Draw the hands on each clock face. The first one has been done for you!

8 o'clock

1 o'clock

3 o'clock

5 o'clock

9 o'clock

7 o'clock

Colour the smiley faces when you've finished!

The Monster in the Lake

Story: Rik Hoskin Art: Nigel Dobbyn

Spider-Man and Doctor Octopus are looking at the interesting pond life at Lake Marvel for their school project.

The Thing and Spider-Girl spend their time skimming stones off the lake's surface. The Thing is very strong and can throw stones much further than Spider-Girl!

Doctor Octopus suddenly spots something in the middle of the lake. "It's a monster," he tells the others.

"Like the one in Loch Ness," Spider-Girl laughs. "This will be the most amazing discovery of the year," Doc Ock says, and he rushes to get a closer look.

The water's too deep for Doc Ock's tentacles. "We need to find some way to get closer," he tells the others.

The Thing has an idea. "We could hop across the lily pads, like a frog," he says. But none of them have jumping powers.

"What if we fly," Doc Ock says, "like the ducks?" But none of them can fly.

"Or we could just float through the water," Spider-Girl says, "like the snails." But that would take too long.

I HOPE IT KEEPS DRY!
Spider-Man uses his special web to make a one-man boat which he will use to cross the lake.
Spidey's boat is a very ancient design called a coracle. Sitting in it is like floating on a big seashell.
WHEE!
sploosh!
The Thing uses his super strength to help Spidey get the boat moving.
NO MONSTERS HERE!
When Spidey reaches the centre of the lake he sees that "the monster" is just an old tree stump, floating in the water.

"It really looked like a monster from a distance," Spidey says, disappointed. "Not to worry," Spider-Girl tells him, "we found lots of other cool animals!"
4

"But I really wanted to see a monster," Spider-Man says. "Maybe next time," the Thing tells him.
The End

Swamped!

There's a monster hiding in the swamp! Can you guide Spider-Man through the maze to find him?

Observation

Spidey's Hospital Dash

Communication

Story: Rik Hoskin Art: Nigel Dobbyn

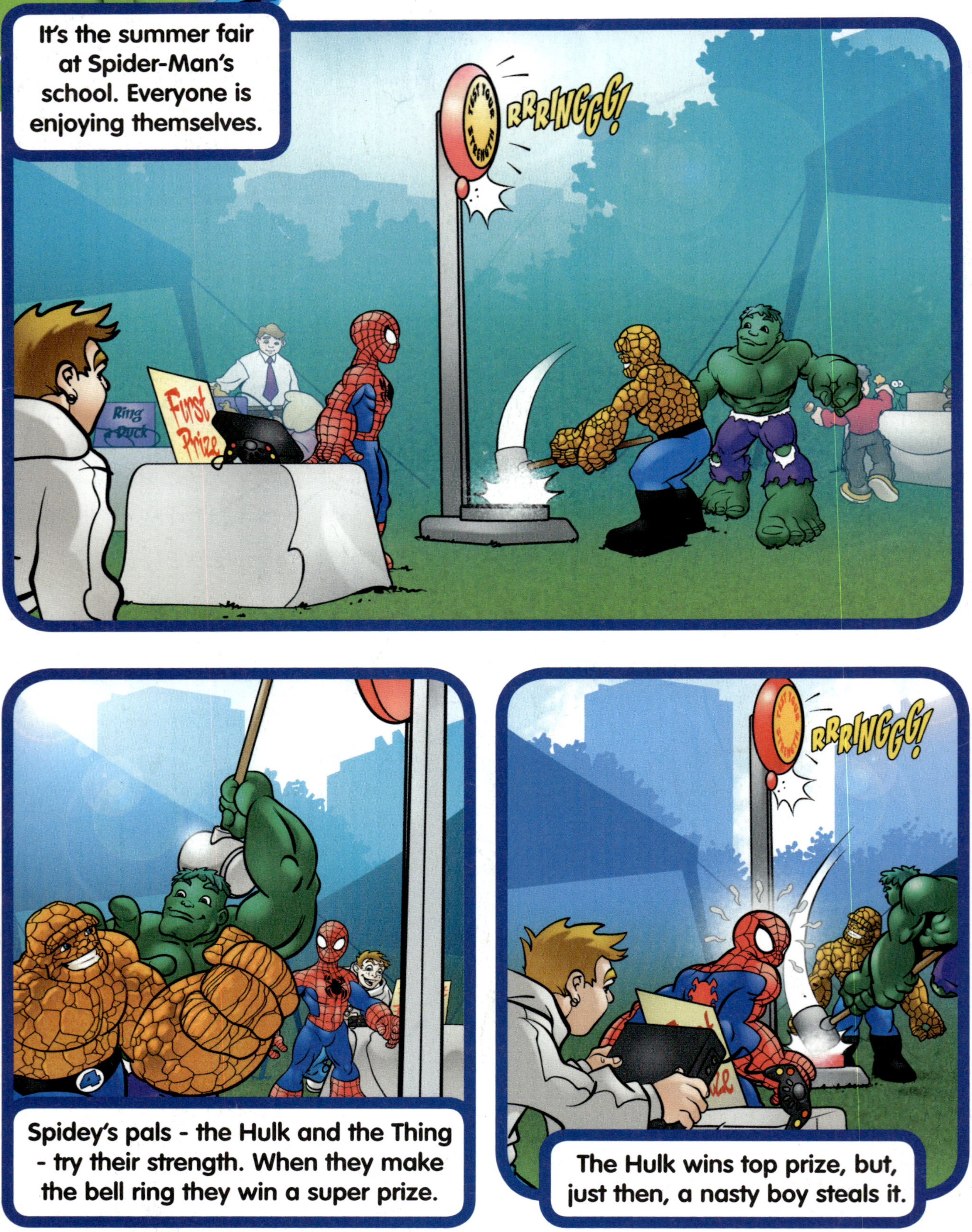

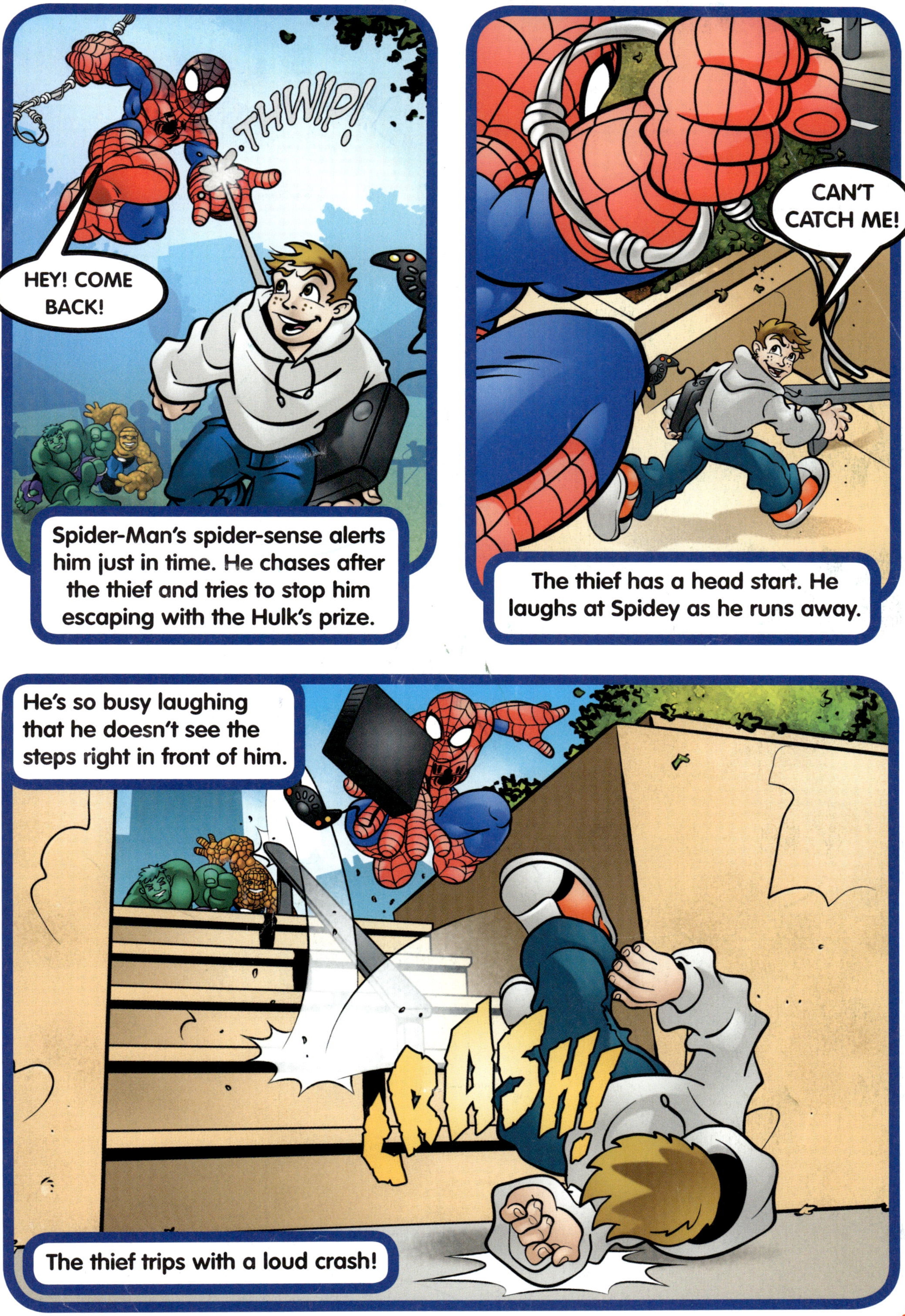
THWIP!
HEY! COME BACK!
Spider-Man's spider-sense alerts him just in time. He chases after the thief and tries to stop him escaping with the Hulk's prize.
CAN'T CATCH ME!
The thief has a head start. He laughs at Spidey as he runs away.
He's so busy laughing that he doesn't see the steps right in front of him.
CRASH!
The thief trips with a loud crash!

MY ARM HURTS!
The thief hurt himself when he fell. "I think you'd better go to the hospital," Spider-Man says.
HOLD ON TIGHT.
The thief feels very foolish when Spider-Man carries him through the park to the hospital. Spidey always tries to help people, even thieves!
HOSPITAL
They are soon at the hospital - a building where lots of doctors work. They'll know how to make the boy feel better.